50p 8-6-2013

C000056278

A selection of Staffordshire pottery figures. Back row: Dick Turpin, c.1850; Queen Victoria, c.1845; middle row: an unidentified theatrical pair, c.1845; the actor John Kemble as Hamlet, c.1870; a spill vase with a milkmaid milking a cow, c.1845; front row: a miniature figure group of a girl and a goat, c.1845; a recumbent spaniel, c.1850.

Staffordshire Figures

1835~1880

Frances Bryant

A Shire book

Published in 2005 by Shire Publications Ltd,
Cromwell House, Church Street, Princes Risborough,
Buckinghamshire HP27 9AA, UK.
(Website: www.shirebooks.co.uk)

Copyright © 2005 by Frances Bryant.
First published 2005.
Shire Album 448. ISBN-10: 0 7478 0636 5;
ISBN-13: 978 0 7478 0636 5.
Frances Bryant is hereby identified as the author of this
work in accordance with Section 77 of the Copyright,
Designs and Patents Act 1988.

All rights reserved. No part of this publication may be
reproduced or transmitted in any form or by any means,
electronic or mechanical, including photocopy, recording,
or any information storage and retrieval system, without
permission in writing from the publishers.

British Library Cataloguing in Publication Data:
Bryant, Frances
Staffordshire figures 1835–1880. – (Shire album; 448)
1. Pottery figures – England – Staffordshire – Collectors
and collecting
2. Staffordshire pottery – Collectors and collecting
I. Title 738.8'2'094246'075
ISBN-10: 0 7478 0636 5.

Cover: *Pair of flatback equestrian portrait figures depicting Prince Albert and Queen Victoria, c.1845.*

ACKNOWLEDGEMENTS
The author would like to thank Ann Boyce for allowing photographs of several fine pieces
to be taken from her private collection. Grateful thanks to Jane Druce for her tireless work
at the computer, typing the manuscript, drawing the map and using all her desktop
publishing skills. Special thanks to Margaret Rooks for supporting all aspects of the
project, and the author! All photographs are the author's own, courtesy of Wessex
Antiques, Sherborne, Dorset.

Note: The measurements given in the book, especially in the captions to the illustrations,
refer to the height of the figure.

Printed in Malta by Gutenberg Press Limited, Gudja Road, Tarxien PLA 19, Malta

Contents

An early Staffordshire figure group modelled 'in the round', such that it can be viewed from any angle, depicting Neptune with a brass trident and seated on a throne in the form of a fish. Note the delicate painting on the fish and shells. c.1835. 15 cm (6 inches).

A charming 'flatback' spill vase, modelled to fit against a wall, and showing all the attributes of a good country wife. She sits next to a beehive, with an enormous tulip behind her, while a curious cat climbs on to her lap after the bird she is cradling. The piece shows the fairly wide range of colours available to the potters. c.1850. 20 cm (8 inches).

Introduction

Victorian Staffordshire figures are unique among ceramic wares as they neatly encapsulate, both socially and historically, the period in which they were produced. They were made by artisans of the new working class

for others in a similar, or only marginally higher, social position. The figures depicted were the popular heroes of the time, royalty and those with power and influence in society, but it was on the mantelpieces of their more humble admirers that they were found. This was because, by the standards of the fine factories such as Chelsea or Derby, Staffordshire figures were mass-produced, crudely modelled and naïvely painted, and much of the subject matter of the potters was deemed unworthy of notice by the great and the good. Not for them the stern gaze of the Nonconformist preacher or notorious criminal. Yet it is their appeal to the Victorian working class that makes the surviving pieces from the many factories of

The potters often depicted figures of topical interest. This portrait figure titled JIMMY WOOD (a spelling error by the potter) shows Jemmy Wood, a Gloucestershire draper who died in 1836 leaving the enormous sum of £781,007 in his will. A wrangle ensued between the City of Gloucester, which believed it had been left £200,000 in a codicil, and his four executors. The city spent over £8000 on legal proceedings, but the House of Lords finally ruled against it in 1844. c.1845. 19 cm (7 1/2 inches).

A flatback spill-vase figure group depicting two children in Highland dress with their dog, seated beside a tree trunk. A train emerges from a brick-built tunnel beneath them. This piece has lovely colouring and is unusual in that the subject was modern for its time. c.1850. 24 cm (9½ inches).

the Staffordshire towns gloriously representative of the subjects that amused, concerned and interested the often illiterate 'common people'.

For the modern collector, Staffordshire figures represent a fascinating snapshot of the Victorian age. They are quirky, fun, sometimes irreverent, and full of character, and they embody in ceramic form the spirit and diversity of the era. It is impossible to include here all the figures made, as unrecorded examples are still coming to light. However, some of the more typical figures which collectors should be able to find without too much difficulty are illustrated in this short guide, as well as a few of the rarer or more unusual pieces.

'The Potteries' and its potters

By 'Staffordshire pottery' we mean the wares that were produced within the area of the six towns of Burslem, Fenton, Hanley, Longton, Stoke and Tunstall that now make up the city of Stoke-on-Trent, known colloquially as 'The Potteries'. Here were many factories, including famous ones such as Wedgwood at the splendid Etruria Works and numerous lesser ones, whose names have become lost to history. The county of Staffordshire was blessed by its natural deposits of clay for modelling and coal for firing, making it an ideal locality for the establishment and growth of the potteries. The so-called 'Staffordshire figures' were generally made by the smaller firms.

Working conditions in these factories or 'potbanks' tended to be harsh, especially in the larger businesses, and the owners unforgiving. Usually hired by the year, a worker at the height of the production period in the mid nineteenth century was paid the weekly rate of a shilling, for children, up to about £3 for an 'oven man', the highest paid and most important position. As workers were paid piece-work this wage was not guaranteed, as figures lost to production through faulty firing or a bad clay mix were docked from their pay, thus giving everyone the incentive to make sure production was successful. The working day was long and hard, usually starting at first light and sometimes lasting well into the

The six towns and main waterways of 'The Potteries'. The area is now the city of Stoke-on-Trent.

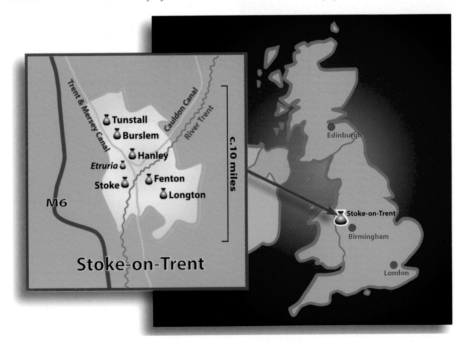

An early photograph showing the pollution caused by the firing of the large 'bottle ovens'. The workers' terraced cottages are very near the workings.

night. Conditions were also dangerous. 'Dippers' would immerse the figures by hand into a liquid lead glaze, which might also contain arsenic. 'Finishers', who sanded off the seams from the newly fired models, created clouds of sharp dust, which they would then inhale, as would their colleagues.

As well as working alongside their male colleagues in most areas of the factories, women and girls were mainly responsible for the decoration of the pieces. The working conditions of the decorators were generally better than those of the other workers: the women sat on high stools close together along workbenches, in a room with large windows for the light by which to paint.

Children as young as five were considered vital to the income of the family. They were often employed by the potters themselves, with no concessions being made to their tender years: they were expected to put in just as long and hard a day's work as their adult masters.

The towns themselves were filthy, noisy places. Black smoke belched from the distinctive 'bottle ovens', obscuring the light of the sun and leaving smutty marks on clothing and buildings. Families – generations of whom could all work in the potteries – would live crowded together in small terraced houses with as many as ten or more people sharing two rooms. Diet was poor, with many people subsisting on bread, potatoes and gruel; any occasional joints of meat were usually saved for the adult males and chief breadwinners of the family, the others having to make do with the scrap ends.

The Gladstone Pottery Museum, the most complete surviving example of a traditional Victorian pottery works (or 'potbank'), showing the cobbled factory yard with the bottle ovens in the background. When in use, this would have been a noisy, industrious area where finished products were packed and dispatched, while raw materials arrived to be processed.

The harsh working conditions were not completely unremitting, however, as potters were allowed Sundays and some other religious holidays off (although these days were unpaid) and conditions gradually improved as the century progressed. Official reports on the conditions in the factories eventually shocked Members of Parliament into passing a number of Education and Factory Acts to improve the lot of the workers, especially the children.

Two early Staffordshire figures with distinctive large-leaved oak trees to the rear, moulded in the round and with a hollow base. Doe, c.1800. 11 cm (4¼ inches). Girl, c.1810. 12 cm (4¾ inches).

The development of the Staffordshire figure

The main period for the production of Staffordshire figures was from the middle of the nineteenth century to its end although figural pieces had been made in this area from the early eighteenth century. Famous potters such as Thomas Whielden (1719–95) made beautiful earthenware figures with 'tortoiseshell' glazes on creamy clay, with browns, greens, blues and yellows often merging into each other. Ralph Wood (1715–72) and his family in turn influenced later potters such as John Walton (c.1780–1835) and Obadiah Sherratt (c.1775–1846). They created figures of classical and bucolic scenes that were painted and modelled 'in the round' (in other words, the pieces are of good colour and modelling when viewed from any angle), often with 'bocage' (leafy excrescences) and stylised large-leaved trees framing the figures. Sheep, lambs and deer mixed with gods, goddesses and muses; there were even bull-baiting groups, as well as busts of religious figures such as John Wesley. William Pratt and his sons continued this tradition during the period 1780–1840 with their distinctive colour palette of high-temperature glazes in greens, blues, oranges, yellows and browns.

All of these potters concentrated on wares that largely followed the styles and tastes preferred by the wealthy and influential. It was only around the time of Victoria's accession to the throne in 1837 that a new type of figure – the recognisable 'Staffordshire figure' – emerged. Staffordshire figures differed in a number of crucial ways from their predecessors. Firstly, their creators gave up trying to emulate the wares of the great factories such as Derby and Chelsea. Secondly, they aimed their production, in both subject matter and style, at a mass market rather than at the select and wealthy few. Thirdly, they did not try to disguise the white clay from which the simple moulds were made.

Production reached its heyday between about 1840 and 1865. These figures are vibrantly coloured, often with the famous cobalt blue which almost defines this period. The range of figures produced was vast, from the ubiquitous 'flatback' figure, with colouring and moulding detail concentrated on the front of the figure, to those modelled in

Above: A Prattware model of 'Charity' holding a baby, with two children standing at her feet. This piece shows a strong classical influence, yet can clearly be seen as a precursor of the Staffordshire figures that were to follow. c.1800. 24 cm (9¹/2 inches).

Finely moulded and painted, this early watch holder is a hybrid piece, where elements of early classicism (the robed figure) meet later elements, such as the solid painted base and the dog. c.1835. 20 cm (8 inches).

the round. They can be purely decorative ornaments or functional pieces, like spill vases, pen holders, watch rests, candle snuffers, pastille burners, stirrup cups and even holy water stoups. They range in height from 2.5 cm (1 inch) to approximately 45 cm (about 18 inches). Care was usually taken with the painting, and models were crisply moulded, some with separately moulded pieces such as legs, arms and sieved-clay bocage that would enliven the basic flatback.

After 1865 the figures could be rather ill defined in moulding and were frequently left largely white, with just gilding or sparse painting to enhance their design. Some manufacturers, such as Thomas Parr, carried

Below left: Showing all the signs of high-quality production, this flatback model of a shepherdess is crisply moulded, beautifully and carefully painted, and colourfully finished. The sheep's coats and 'bocage' (flora) have been made by applying sieved clay to the figure before firing. c.1850. 28 cm (11 inches).

Below right: The rear of the shepherdess shows a typical flatback. The figure was meant to stand against a wall, being viewed only from the front.

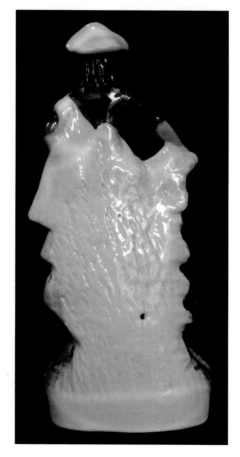

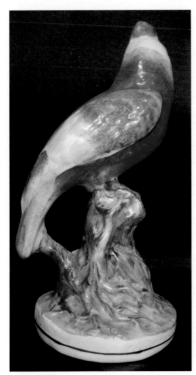

The rear of a parrot figure, showing modelling 'in the round'. This piece has been moulded and coloured all round and may be viewed from any angle. The front of the figure is shown on page 38. c.1850. 23 cm (9 inches).

on producing sought-after figures with modelling and colouring in the round into the 1870s. His factories were later taken over by William Kent, who continued production into the twentieth century. There are also some fine figures of generals dating from the 1880s and 1890s, but by and large production in terms of both quantity and quality was in decline.

By the time of Victoria's death in 1901 the art had almost died out, with only a few new figures being made, and these were often pale imitations of figures that had appeared at the height of production in the nineteenth century.

Relatively little is known of the names of the potters who produced these wares, and the figures themselves

A pair of equestrian flatback figures showing the later vogue for minimal decoration: although the piece is well modelled, only the skin, hair and gilding decorate the basic white of the clay. One hardly notices the stag thrown over the front of the figure! c.1870. 37 cm (14¹/₂ inches).

A Parr/Kent figure of a strolling minstrel, well modelled in the round with colouring that echoes earlier periods of production. c.1875. 23 cm (9 inches).

are almost never marked. James Dudson made some fine animals and flatback wares, as did John and Rebecca Lloyd, whose figures were impress-marked LLOYD SHELTON on the base or back. Sampson Smith (1813–78) is probably the best-documented maker of flatback groups; with some of his original moulds having been discovered, it is known that he was responsible for a number of important figures. Fred Archer, the jockey, Highland Mary, and Moody and Sankey, the American evangelists, have all been attributed to him. Some of his figures are marked S (or SAMPSON) SMITH, LONGTON.

Production methods

A typical Staffordshire figure was made using a two-part plaster 'press mould' comprising a front and a back and cast from an original clay model. A piece or 'bat' of body clay was rolled flat and then pressed by hand firmly into each half of the mould, and the rough edges were trimmed to create a flat bonding edge. Both edges were brushed with liquid clay ('slip') and the mould was bound together by cord. It was then left to dry in a heated room, which caused it to shrink slightly away from the mould, enabling its easy removal. Slip moulds were occasionally used in this period: slip was poured into the mould, left to dry, and excess slip was poured away to leave a figure that was slightly less well defined and lighter. The plaster moulds were re-used over and over again but would gradually wear out, so that figures made from later pressings lack some of the crisp definition found in those of earlier pressings.

The base was stuck on with slip and, if more complicated sections were required, such as arms, paws, separate legs or extruded foliage, these were also added at this stage. More complicated figures were thus more time-consuming to produce and therefore more expensive. A small hole was made in the base or back of the figure to allow for the expansion of air otherwise trapped within when fired. Finished figures often show 'firing cracks', where the air has forced its own way out, sometimes along the mould joins.

The figure was then given a first or 'biscuit' firing in the biscuit oven at 1100°C, emerging brittle and porous and ready for the under-glaze colours. There were only two colours able to withstand the heat of the

A view of the interior of a figure through the (broken) base. Here, the finger marks of the potter can clearly be seen where the wet clay was pressed into the mould. At the top right, white glaze has seeped through a crack where the two pieces meet.

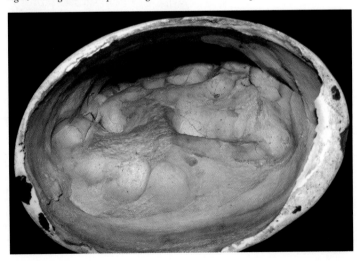

A flatback group of an unidentified boy and girl in a 'seahorse' boat. The rich cobalt blue has been applied too thickly and has run – a charming figure nonetheless. c.1855. 20 cm (8 inches).

A flatback spill-vase figure of a couple by a flowing well. No cobalt blue has been used but note the insipid blue for the bodice laces and on the bow belt. The line of gilding round the base and spill rim is from liquid gold, which gives a harsh colour. Despite this, the figure is well moulded and has good colour. c.1865. 20 cm (8 inches).

An unusual and comic flatback spill vase showing two gentlemen dancing around a camp fire. c.1850. 16 cm (6¼ inches).

glaze, or 'glost', oven: the dazzling, deep cobalt blue most associated with Staffordshire figures, and black. The blue was made from cobalt manganese and the black from iron oxides. Cobalt, which was relatively expensive and dangerous to apply, was used only in the heyday, until about 1865, when a more insipid over-glaze blue became available. After the under-glaze colours had been applied the figure was fired in the glost oven at around 650°C to harden the colours. It was then dipped into a tank of clear lead glaze (or glost), after which it would go for its third firing, again in the glost oven, but at 950°C, so that the figure was completely sealed.

Next, over-glaze enamel colours were painted on, using a cheerful but fairly limited palette of black, yellow, pink, orange, green and brown. Gilding would also be applied to finish off the decoration, using gold powder mixed with 'flux' (a melting agent) to produce a 'soft' gold colour upon firing. After around 1860 liquid gold was increasingly used, which gives a much harsher, brighter look. Both forms of gilding tend to rub off with age and frequent handling.

Finally, the figure was given its fourth and final firing, at 850°C, to fix the colours.

Figure of General Charles Gordon (1833–85), hero of the Sudan War, who was killed during the Siege of Khartoum. This figure is a later model with sparse colouring and is from a well-used mould, as the definition is poor. Nevertheless, it remains a popular and collectable military piece. c.1885. 44 cm (17 ¾ inches).

The figures

During their period of production the Staffordshire factories produced many thousands of figures covering an enormous range of subjects. The potters aimed to capture the popular interests and concerns of the mainly urban working class and so figures were modelled on many topical

subjects popular with the masses. Often they are based on illustrations from contemporary pamphlets or newspapers and popular prints and could be produced rapidly in order to exploit fully the news stories of the day.

Royalty

Queen Victoria and her large family provided rich inspiration for the potters and popular figures for her loyal subjects to collect. She was modelled alone, or with Prince Albert – either as one figure or, more usually, as a pair of separate figures. Most of their nine children were also the subjects of many of the models, especially the Princess Royal (born in 1840) and the Prince of Wales (born in

Above: An equestrian flatback portrait figure of Queen Victoria on a prancing horse. The gilt script on the base reads 'Queen' and the figure forms one half of a pair with the Prince Consort, Albert. c.1850. 27 cm (10¹/₂ inches).

Right: A portrait figure of Prince Albert sitting on a chair draped with ermine and holding papers. This figure would have been paired with a similar Queen Victoria. c.1845. 15 cm (6 inches).

A miniature portrait figure group of Queen Victoria and Prince Albert, he in colourful uniform jacket. These miniature figures were sometimes given away as 'fairings' (small presents given, or won, at fairs). c.1850. 9.5 cm (3³/4 inches).

Above: *A flatback portrait group of the young Prince of Wales on a pony. This figure can be mistaken for the Princess Royal, with which it is paired (not shown), as the Prince is wearing a dress, but this was the custom for young Victorian children, whether boys or girls. The more masculine collar and short hair are indications of his gender. c.1846. 15 cm (6 inches).*

The Princess Royal as a young girl, here modelled with a bird. Her long hair and collarless neckline emphasise her gender. c.1848. 16 cm (6¹/4 inches).

1841). As the children grew to adulthood and married into the royal families of Europe more models were created to celebrate engagements and weddings. Foreign sovereigns linked to the affairs of Britain appeared with regularity throughout the period. The Crimean War of 1854–6 inspired a figure of Queen Victoria flanked by Sultan Abd-ul-Medjid of Turkey and Napoleon III of France.

Soldiers, admirals and politicians

The Duke of Wellington was modelled both as the victor of Waterloo in 1815 and in his later political role; his enemy Napoleon was also depicted in many models, and both can be found in a variety of sizes. The great and enduringly popular naval commander Admiral Lord Nelson was featured in numerous poses, including that of his famous death scene on board HMS *Victory* at the Battle of Trafalgar in 1805.

The Queen was head of an empire that spanned the globe. During times of war or uprising, great popular heroes emerged – fuelling the nation's patriotism and engendering the craze for 'portrait figures'. The

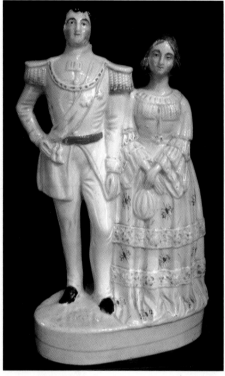

A flatback portrait group of the Princess Royal and Prince Frederick III of Prussia to celebrate their marriage in 1858. 30 cm (12 inches).

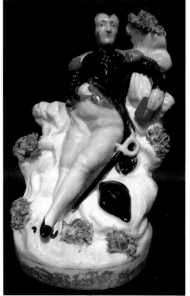

An unusual, beautifully modelled and painted portrait figure, probably representing the defeated Napoleon on St Helena. He sits in military uniform on a bank, his left hand holding a book, his sword and hat nearby, while gazing wistfully into the distance. c.1845. 20 cm (8 inches).

Three portrait figures of the Duke of Wellington, reflecting his early role as a great military leader and his later role as the nation's leading politician. (Clockwise from top left) A small flatback of Wellington as a young man, in full military uniform, c.1845, 16 cm (6¹/2 inches); a 'Toby' jug moulded as a bust of Wellington in military dress, c.1845, 17 cm (6³/4 inches); a flatback of Wellington in civilian dress with 'Wellington' in gilt script at the base, c.1850, 34 cm (13¹/2 inches). In the second and third examples the potters have taken considerable trouble to capture Wellington's distinctive features.

Crimean War, in which Britain and France declared war on Russia in response to its invasion of Turkey, gave rise to numerous examples. The army commanders Field Marshal Lord Raglan, who died in 1855, and General Sir James Simpson (in a pair with General Sir Charles Windham) made striking figures, as did the commander of the Baltic Fleet, Admiral Sir Charles Napier, and Admiral Sir James Dundas. The heroism of the lower ranks was celebrated in figures like 'The Wounded Soldier', 'The Soldier's Return' and 'The Soldier's Farewell'. Florence Nightingale was also celebrated for her care of wounded soldiers at Scutari.

Figures of Victoria's most famous prime ministers can also be found – Robert Peel, William Gladstone and Benjamin Disraeli.

The Indian Mutiny of 1857–9 inspired a number of figures, particularly General Sir Henry Havelock, General Sir Colin Campbell and the unlikely figure of 'Highland Jessie', who, although merely the wife of a lowly corporal at the siege of Lucknow in 1857, inspired the entire garrison to hold out by

Above: *A flatback portrait figure of Admiral Sir James Dundas, a naval commander of the Crimean War. c.1854. 33 cm (13 inches).*

A flatback Crimean War figure group showing a soldier leaning on his sailor companion. Gilded lettering on the base reads 'The Wounded Soldier'. c.1855. 25 cm (10 inches).

Two small Crimean War patriotic figures, one showing a girl welcoming home a returning sailor, the other a girl with a flag and drum. Both c.1855. 13 cm (5 inches).

claiming to hear the pipes of the relieving forces coming closer.

Foreign exploits often caught the popular imagination. The liberation of Italy in 1870 inspired several figures of Garibaldi after his triumphant march into Rome with a small band of followers. The Franco-Prussian War of the same year gave rise to figures of the Prussian King William I and his powerful Chancellor, Bismarck, as well as to figures of Marshall MacMahon and Marshall Bazaine, the French commanders.

The trend for portrait figures continued up to the Egyptian and Sudan campaigns of 1882–98 and the Boer War of 1899–1902, and these campaigns inspired some of the best-modelled figures of the later period, such as

A flatback equestrian figure of General Sir Henry Havelock, the commander of the British forces in the Indian Mutiny. Note the early use of sparse colouring on this figure. c.1858. 28 cm (11 inches).

General Gordon and Lord Kitchener. By this time, however, figure production was already in decline.

Religious and mythological

Nothing better illustrates the target market for Staffordshire figures than the religious subjects that were chosen for modelling. Nonconformity was popular with many working people and figures were made of John Wesley, the American evangelists Moody and Sankey, and the Reverend Charles Spurgeon. Many Catholic households had figures of Pope Pius IX and Cardinal Manning, the Archbishop of Westminster, and there were holy water stoups with representations of Christ on the cross. Scenes and figures from the Old and New Testaments were also modelled.

Below left: A flatback portrait figure of Dwight Lyman Moody, an American evangelist, one of a pair with Ira David Sankey (not illustrated). He stands by a pedestal, his right hand resting on the Bible; the name MOODY *is in raised script at the base. c.1873. 30 cm (12 inches).*

Below right: A flatback holy water stoup showing Christ on the cross with attendant putti and symbolic fruiting vine. This figure was made for the immigrant Catholic market comprising the thousands who arrived on the west coast of England after the Irish potato famine of the 1840s. c.1850. 28 cm (11 inches).

A flatback spill vase depicting the Old Testament story in which Rebecca gives a drink of water to the servant at the well; both wear brightly painted Eastern-style costume. c.1850. 27 cm (10¹/₂ inches).

Mythological subjects were also represented, including figures of Neptune, the Roman god of the sea, and – in a patriotic age of Empire – of Britannia, the personification of the spirit of the British Isles.

The arts and literature

Both contemporary and historical authors and poets were depicted, as well as many characters from their plays and novels. Even the actors and actresses who brought them to life were depicted, often as melodramatic figures captured in a typical pose.

Several Shakespearean figures illustrate this trend well, with many models produced from plays such as *Romeo and Juliet, Hamlet, Henry V* and *Richard III*, together with the

Left: An early figure of a bust of the Roman god Neptune, this example left uncoloured. He wears a cape of fish skins. c.1830. 35 cm (13¹/₂ inches).

A beautifully shaped and painted figure of Britannia, modelled in the round. She sits on a faux marble base holding a brass trident, a shield with a crude Union Jack design at her side, and a recumbent lion at her feet. c.1870. 37 cm (14¹/₂ inches).

A strongly coloured flatback portrait figure of William Shakespeare dressed in flowing robe and leaning on a book-topped plinth as he points to his manuscript. c.1850. 18 cm (7 inches).

actors who played the title roles: David Garrick, William Macready and the actress Isabella Glyn, who was famous for her role as Lady Macbeth. A pensive Shakespeare was also modelled as a Staffordshire figure. Other popular figures include Robert Burns, John Milton, Sir Walter Scott and Lord Byron, and characters from Dickens – Mr Pickwick, and David Copperfield with Clara Peggotty.

Music, particularly popular opera and music hall, was an important working-class entertainment of the period. The

A flatback bower group of Romeo and Juliet. Although sparsely coloured, the model has been sensitively painted to show the lovers' adoration of one another. c.1850. 20 cm (8 inches).

A well-coloured flatback portrait figure of the actor David Garrick as Richard III, leaning on a couch in his campaign tent. The image was taken from a popular engraving of the time. c.1850. 24 cm (9¹/₂ inches).

From Sir Walter Scott's novel 'Rob Roy', a figure of the character Diana Vernon dressed in decorative equestrian attire and holding a riding crop. c.1850. 30 cm (12 inches).

Following the popularity of the American Christian emancipation novel 'Uncle Tom's Cabin' by Harriet Beecher Stowe, this beautifully painted piece shows Eva perched on Tom's knee. Figures from popular literature were common as reading was a pleasurable pastime for many Victorians. 'Uncle Tom's Cabin' had also aroused much sympathy for the slaves of the Southern states in the period of the American Civil War (1861–5). 26 cm (10 inches).

singer Jenny Lind (known as 'the Swedish Nightingale') was represented, and Paul and Virginie – figures from Lesueur's popular opera – made a striking pair. Myriad unnamed musicians and dancers were also produced.

Figures from children's tales such as *Little Red Riding Hood* and *The Babes in the Wood* were ever popular. Circus performers included lion tamers and bareback riders. Even Jumbo, the elephant who was killed when charging a

Right: A flatback spill vase showing Jenny Lind in the role of Marie and Luigi LaBlanche as Sergeant Sulpice. She stands under an arching tree bough to salute the drum-carrying sergeant. c.1847. 13 cm (5¼ inches).

Below: A pair of flatback figures depicting characters from the popular eighteenth-century opera 'Paul et Virginie'. Virginie sits holding a nest with eggs, and Paul holds a bird aloft. An axe lies nearby. c.1850. 34 cm (13½ inches).

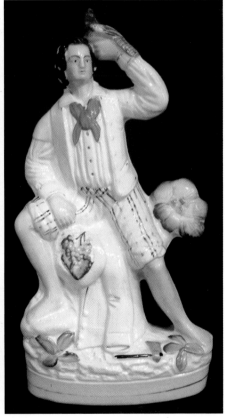

A flatback spill vase with Little Red Riding Hood sitting by a tree trunk with a basket of goodies while a somewhat foxy-looking wolf gazes up at her. Little Red Riding Hood's cloak is orange as the potters were unable to produce a true red colour with their over-glaze enamels. c.1850. 23 cm (9¹/₂ inches).

Below: *Two representations of the popular children's tale 'Babes in the Wood'. In the figure on the left, a flatback spill vase, a guardian angel and robin stand guard over the sleeping children. c.1845. 16 cm (6¹/₄ inches). In the other, the children sleep beneath a bower made by a fruiting vine. c.1860. 16 cm (6¹/₄ inches).*

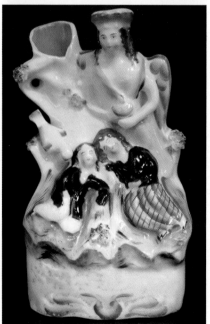

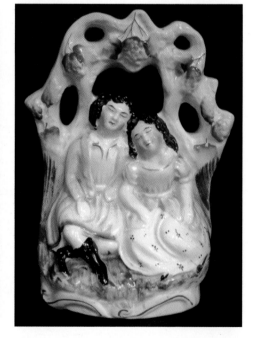

Above left: *A flatback portrait figure of the popular stage performer Thomas Potter Cooke in his role as Ben Backstay. Dressed as a sailor, he stands cross-legged, a purse held aloft and a straw boater in his right hand. c.1850. 20 cm (8 inches).*

Above right: *A flatback theatrical figure group of an unidentified couple in costume, he with an ermine-lined robe and she with a stringed instrument. c.1850. 17 cm (6¾ inches).*

Left: *From the eighteenth-century opera 'Artaxerxes' by Thomas Arne, the figure of Mandane, modelled in the round. She sits playing a lute and is dressed in Eastern costume. c.1845. 18 cm (7 inches).*

stationary railway carriage while he was being transported to another show by the American circus-owner P. T. Barnum, was turned into a Staffordshire figure.

Heroes and villains

Explorers and adventurers were popular heroes as the horizons of the Victorian world continued to expand. Adventurers included Sir John Franklin, who died in 1847 searching in Arctic seas for the North-West Passage, and Roualeyn George Gordon Cumming, the Lion Slayer, whose

A flatback figure group which, although untitled, is thought to represent Roualeyn George Gordon Cumming, the Lion Slayer. He stands holding a gun, his faithful dog by his side. c.1852. 34 cm (13¹/2 inches).

book, *Five Years of a Hunter's Life in the Far Interior of Africa*, was an instant success. At a time when nationalism was extolled, certain romantic historical heroes were also popular, such as Sir William Wallace, the Scottish patriot who resisted the English at the end of the thirteenth century.

Sporting heroes were celebrated in pottery, from the rare cricketing groups thought to represent the batsmen Julius Caesar, Fuller Pilch and Thomas Box, the wicket-keeper George Parr and the round-arm bowler Frederick William Lillywhite. There are even rarer models of the boxers Carmel Heenan and Tom Sayers, who fought one of the last bare-

A large flatback portrait figure of Sir William Wallace, the Scottish patriot and hero. It has subtle colours with WALLACE *in raised gilt script at the base. c.1860. 44 cm (17¹/2 inches).*

A flatback equestrian portrait group, which, although untitled, is widely believed to be of Fred Archer, the champion jockey. c.1860. 22 cm (8½ inches).

knuckle bouts in 1860. Jockey figures are thought to be modelled on Fred Archer, a champion jockey who rode almost two and a half thousand winners.

The modellers also delighted in representing the less salubrious side of society with figures commemorating notorious criminals. The most infamous of these were the eighteenth-century highwaymen Dick Turpin and Tom King but a whole series of figures associated with contemporary crimes could be collected. In 1848, for example, James Bloomfield Rush of Potash Farm murdered his creditor Isaac Jermy and his son-in-law. Rush appears as one of a pair with the woman who gave evidence against him, his mistress Emily Sandford, and the buildings associated with the crime are also modelled – Potash Farm, Stanfield Hall (the

A matched pair of flatback equestrian portrait figures of the highwaymen Dick Turpin and Tom King, one with D. TURPIN in painted black raised letters to the base, the other with TOM KING in raised gilt letters. Both c.1850, 26 cm (10 inches).

A flatback group of two colourfully clad fisherwomen, a basket by their side. The potters have managed to convey great character in this charming piece. c.1865. 23 cm (9 inches).

home of Jermy), and Norwich Castle, where Rush was hanged and buried.

Rural life

Ordinary tasks and seasonal occupations feature in numerous models depicting the rural life abandoned by the new working classes as they moved into the heavily industrialised towns. Harvesters, milk-maids, fisher-folk, gardeners, hunters, shepherds and shepherdesses and children were all represented, as were the idealised cottages in which they lived. The cottages were often moulded as pastille burners to hold a scented paste 'pastille' that was burnt to mask the unpleasant odours of the urban street. Watch holders held father's precious pocket-watch when he returned from work; spill vases, generally modelled as tree

A miniature pair of a sailor and his lady standing by mooring pillars wound around with thick rope. The figures show good, detailed modelling, which is often lacking in miniature pieces. c.1845. 9.5 cm (3³/4 inches).

A colourful spill-vase group showing three children with a book and a yellow cradle at their feet. c.1850. 16 cm (6¹/4 inches).

Right: *A jolly little pastille burner in the form of a Gothic lodge, its overhanging roof supported by rustic pillars, with bocage and brightly painted flowers. c.1850. 10 cm (4 inches).*

A flatback turreted castle with a central clock-tower and copious bocage. It is similar to a model entitled 'Norwich Castle', where the notorious James Rush was hanged for murder. c.1850. 14 cm (5¹/2 inches).

A large, striking flatback model of a turreted house with a central clock. Below the house a water bird swims along a stream. c.1860. 33 cm (13 inches).

trunks with the spills as branches, pen holders, cow creamers (cream jugs in the shape of a cow) and cruet sets were all produced in a huge variety of designs and styles.

Animals

Most people associate Staffordshire pottery with the flatback spaniel dogs often found sitting on the mantelpiece of an elderly relative. Thousands of these 'mantel dogs' – often known as 'comforter spaniels' – were made, more than any other type of figure, their popularity enduring as the spaniel was one of the Royal Family's favourite breeds. Red and white, black and white, even green or blue and white, as well as the common gilt and white, were produced – and not just in the usual flatback seated pose. Working dogs were also popular: greyhounds with rabbits, game-retrieving water poodles with clipped and sieved clay coats, Dalmatians, lurchers and even Saint Bernards were produced, while pugs

These handsome 'red' and white flatback spaniels are typical of the 'comforter' spaniels that proudly sat on many Victorian mantelpieces. Although many thousands were produced, they are becoming increasingly hard to find in good condition and in their original pairs. c.1860. 25 cm (10 inches).

Left: *A more unusual flatback figure of two spaniels sitting with a barrel, not in the traditional 'comforter' spaniel pose. c.1850. 20 cm (8 inches).*

Above: *A pen holder modelled as a recumbent greyhound, an attractive ornament for a writing desk. c.1845. 10 cm (4 inches).*

Left: *A pair of large poodle figures. Their separately modelled front legs and chip-glazed coats were added to the basic two-part mould by hand, thus making them more expensive and time-consuming to produce. c.1860. 25 cm (10 inches).*

A pair of Dalmatian dogs, well modelled in the round, their tails curled over their backs. c.1865. 16 cm (6¹/4 inches).

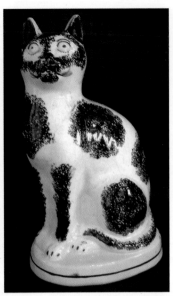

Above left: A flatback spill vase sensitively modelled as an Italian greyhound. The modeller has captured the character of the breed, giving this piece a naturalistic quality. c.1855. 18 cm (7 inches).

Above right: An extremely rare model of a sponged black and white cat, which stands 25 cm (10 inches) high, much taller than most other cat figures. c.1850.

and Italian greyhounds feature as popular companion dogs.

Some of the rarest models depict the most common domestic animals. Cats were thought of as a means of controlling vermin rather than as pets until late in the nineteenth century, and domestic rabbits were a source

A rare pair of miniature Staffordshire cats, with sponged decoration. Cats are uncommon, so finding a pair adds even more to the desirability and value of the figures. c.1840. 7.5 cm (3 inches).

Left: *A miniature crouching rabbit with dramatic black and white colouring. c.1850. 5 cm (2 inches).*

Right: *Unusual cow creamer with the cow in sponged black decoration and a milkmaid attendant. Milk enters through a hole in the maid's hat and pours through the cow's open mouth – the milkmaid also serving as a handle. c.1875. 18.5 cm (7¹/4 inches).*

of food, and their wild counterparts vermin, so few figures of these creatures were made.

Wild creatures such as swans, deer and occasionally foxes and squirrels were produced. Farm animals such as horses, donkeys, cows and chickens (especially the two-piece moulded hens on their nest to hold eggs) proved popular – perhaps to remind the new town dwellers of their lost rural life. Sheep with 'chip-glazed' coats were also made: to achieve the woolly

A pair of spill vases of a ram and ewe with chip-glazed coats. c.1870. 13 cm (5¹/4 inches).

A delicately moulded stirrup cup in the form of a fox head. This piece illustrates the quality that the potters could achieve, although it would have cost a matter of pennies. c.1845. Length 14 cm (5¹/₂ inches).

A flatback spill vase with two swans in front of a tree trunk with much brightly painted bocage. c.1850. 11 cm (4¹/₄ inches).

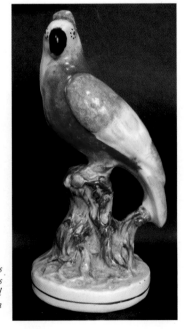

A colourful parrot figure modelled in the round. Victorian society was entranced by the discoveries of the great British explorers, and figures such as this represented the exotic creatures described by the intrepid travellers. The rear of this figure is shown on page 12. c.1850. 23 cm (9 inches).

A flatback spill vase with a handsome and rare lion, showing good-quality painting and modelling. c.1850. 17 cm (6¾ inches).

Very few of Victoria's subjects had seen a real zebra and, in order to save costs and production time, some potters used horse moulds and simply painted stripes on to the figures. This is shown in the figure on the left, which is striped, despite its full mane and bridle. In contrast, the other figure has been modelled as a more lifelike zebra, with an upright short, striped mane and no reins. Both styles are highly collectable and relatively rare. c.1850.

A striking flatback spill-vase group, depicting a zebra in full flight chased by a rather European-looking fox-like animal. The modellers knew little about Africa as the continent was in the process of being opened up by European explorers, so they were untroubled by the zoological inaccuracies of their pieces. c.1850. 26 cm (10 inches).

texture the potters would apply a layer of finely sieved pottery over the body, which was then glazed.

More exotic animals caught the public imagination, particularly those from newly explored areas of the British Empire, which provided adventurous subject matter for the potter looking for a new 'best-seller'. Brightly coloured birds, lions, leopards and zebras (sometimes taken from the mould for a horse) can be found.

Fakes and forgeries

When purchasing Staffordshire figures it is very important to realise that there are many fakes, copies and even forgeries on the market, ranging from the disconcertingly effective to the downright hideously obvious. The task of identification is made even harder by the fact that quite a number of figures were re-cast in the 1950s from their original Victorian moulds. However, the colours of these figures are slightly wrong and there is often a chalky feel to the base.

There is no definitive way to tell a fake piece from a genuine one, but rather a series of pointers that taken individually, or in combination, can help the confused buyer. Please note that the following are general rules and that there will always be some exceptions.

Weight

Most figures should be fairly weighty for their size. This is because press clay moulds rather than slip moulds were usually used. Many modern pieces are made using slip moulds and are consequently smoother in appearance and lighter in weight. They also lack crispness of definition.

Colour

There was a fairly limited range of colours from which the potters could choose. For example, a true red colour is never seen. Bear in mind that cobalt blue was always under-glaze colour and its true intensity is difficult to reproduce.

Above: The bases of figures should be unmarked except for the occasional moulded mould number (especially common on 'comforter' spaniels) or a small mark made by the painter – here shown as an orange dash.

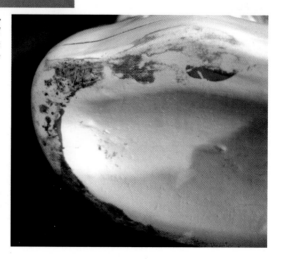

The base of a late production figure or a reproduction figure; these were often made from an original mould. Because the figure has not been fully immersed in the glaze, the base edges are unglazed and have a distinctive chalky feel.

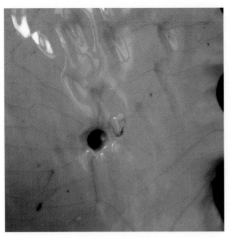

A typical small air hole in the back (or sometimes base) of a figure.

Air holes

There should be a small air hole, no wider than 8 mm (just over ¹/₄ inch) in the base or back of the figure, to enable heated gases to escape during firing. Remember that in spill vases, pen holders and similar pieces there will be no need for this as the natural hole provided by function will suffice. Despite the potter's precaution, air might sometimes still force its way through 'firing cracks', jagged-edged splits of varying lengths that can be seen *under* the glaze. Unsophisticated reproductions do not have these.

Glazing cracks

Sometimes the glazing on figures would crack over time, creating myriad little squares and lined patterns. This effect can be reproduced but it is often done too obviously, with the squares being too similar in size to each other. In genuine Staffordshire pieces *it is only the glazing that should be crazed, not the pottery underneath.* Sometimes badly faked pieces have fake glazing cracks drawn directly on the pottery, underneath the perfectly crack-free glaze.

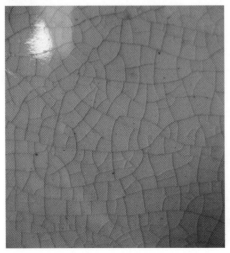

A typical pattern of cracks, which are in the glaze, not the pottery. They are fairly irregular and produce very fine lines. This cracking is not present on every piece, so do not take its absence as an indication of a reproduction figure.

A spaniel dog jug showing some paint chips in the over-glaze enamel colours, revealing the glazed white base colour beneath. Chips such as these occur on most Victorian figures.

A firing crack with indicative ragged edges, showing where the air has forced its way through a seam at the firing stage. Even pieces with fairly severe cracks were not discarded, as they might be in a modern factory, but were merely painted over.

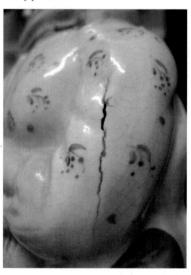

Paint chips

The over-glaze paints used on Victorian pieces often look fairly matt against the shiny under-glaze colours. Sometimes, when paint was thickly applied, it chipped off, revealing the glazed white pottery underneath. The copies rarely have these characteristic white chips.

Attribution

Apart from the handful of figures with maker's marks, the vast majority of Victorian figures should have no form of printing or impressed mark to their underside. No period figure should have 'Staffordshire' or 'Made in Staffordshire' printed on its base. Sometimes dogs have a moulded number on their base, or there will be a small mark made by the painter, such as a dot or line, but anything else should be disregarded.

There is no substitute for handling the figures and familiarising yourself with the colour palette, weight, glaze and so on. The golden rule is: *If in doubt, do not buy.*

Notes for collectors

Heeding the warnings of the previous chapter, those who are unsure of their ground would be well advised to go to a reputable dealer. Dealers should always issue a receipt detailing the age and authenticity of a piece, with a clear indication of whether any restoration has occurred. Walk away from any dealer who shows a reluctance to give such a guarantee.

For those with more experience, auctions and less-specialised dealers can also be a good source of figures, as can antique fairs.

Figures in perfect condition, being the most sought after, will attract a premium in price. These, however, are becoming increasingly difficult to find. Although it is always best to purchase perfect pieces, it is not always possible, especially with rarer figures. Here, good restoration is acceptable, but avoid at all costs poor or slap-dash restoration because, as with any other antique, bad restoration can cause more damage than leaving a piece damaged and unrestored.

Minor paint-chipping and firing cracks are not serious and are only to be expected on older pieces.

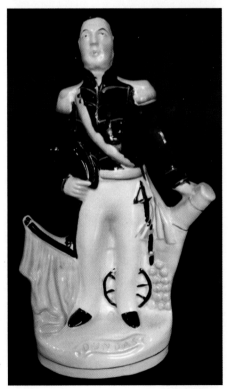

A flatback portrait figure of Sir James Dundas which, when compared with the same model on page 21, shows a marked loss of definition, especially in the face. The poorer definition indicates that the figure is from a later pressing. Several moulds would be made of the most popular figures to ensure that a good quality of production was maintained.

One of the attractive aspects of Staffordshire figures is that, although they were mass-produced, they were all painted individually by hand. This gives each one its own unique character. Here are two portrait heads resulting from identical moulds of the Duke of Wellington; they are equally well moulded but have been painted differently, one suggesting a more youthful man, the other an older statesman, thus subtly altering the tone of the piece.

When purchasing any piece you should always take into account the following:

Colour – is it good and has it been well applied?

Condition – unrestored is best but good restoration is perfectly acceptable as long as it is of high quality, properly explained, and reflected in a lower price.

Crispness of moulding – the moulding on the piece should be clear and well defined: pieces that were produced from old moulds lack definition, appear smoother, and can often lose some features altogether.

Appeal – most importantly of all, does the piece fit all the criteria that make you want to live with it for many years to come? Quite simply, *do you like it?*

Whether you are an avid collector or just want the occasional piece, Victorian Staffordshire figures still represent a relatively affordable way to own a real piece of Victorian history.

Further reading

Balston, Thomas. *Staffordshire Portrait Figures of the Victorian Age*. Faber, 1958.

Harding, Adrian and Nicholas. *Victorian Staffordshire Figures 1835–1875* (three volumes). Schiffer, 1998.

Mason-Pope, Clive. *A–Z of Staffordshire Dogs: A Potted History*. Antique Collectors' Club, 1990.

Oliver, Anthony. *The Victorian Staffordshire Figure*. Heinemann, 1971.

Pugh, P. D. Gordon. *Staffordshire Portrait Figures*. Antique Collectors' Club, 1987.

Sekers, David. *The Potteries*. Shire, 1981; reprinted 2000.

A cruet in the form of a 'Toby', a rotund figure clutching a mug of ale. The centre of his hat lifts off to reveal a glazed interior and the hat brim acts as a pouring lip for vinegar or oil. c.1850. 15 cm (6 inches).

Places to visit

Before travelling, visitors are advised to find out the opening times of museums, and also to confirm that items of interest will be on show.

Ashmolean Museum of Art and Archaeology, Beaumont Street, Oxford OX1 2PH. Telephone: 01865 278000. Website: www.ashmol.ox.ac.uk

Brighton Museum and Art Gallery, Royal Pavilion Gardens, Brighton, East Sussex BN1 1EE. Telephone: 01273 290900. Website: www.brighton.virtualmuseum.info (The Willett Collection)

The Fitzwilliam Museum, Trumpington Street, Cambridge CB2 1RB. Telephone: 01223 332900. Website: www.fitzmuseum.cam.ac.uk

The Nelson Museum, New Market Hall, Priory Street, Monmouth, Monmouthshire NP5 3XA. Telephone: 01600 713519. Website: www.monmouth.org.uk/History/nelson

The Potteries Museum and Art Gallery, Bethesda Street, Hanley, Stoke-on-Trent, Staffordshire ST1 3DW. Telephone: 01782 232323. Website: www2002.stoke.gov.uk/museums

Royal Naval Museum, HM Naval Base (PP66), Portsmouth, Hampshire PO1 3NH. Telephone: 023 9272 7562. Website: www.royalnavalmuseum.org (Nelson and some naval figures)

The Victoria and Albert Museum, Cromwell Road, South Kensington, London SW7 2RL. Telephone: 020 7942 2000. Website: www.vam.ac.uk

Index